TAJ MAHAL

A Visitor's Guide

*Illustrated with
40 full-colour
photographs by R. K. Bose*

BIKRAM GREWAL

HEINEMANN : LONDON

William Heinemann Ltd
10 Upper Grosvenor Street, London W1X 9PA

LONDON MELBOURNE TORONTO
JOHANNESBURG AUCKLAND

First published 1986
© Text and photographs, Dass Media PVT Ltd 1986
SBN 434 30580 4

Printed in Hong Kong by
Imago Publishing Limited

The builder could not have been of
this earth for it is evident the
design was given him by heaven

Shah Jahan

The Taj Mahal dedicated to Mumtaz Mahal

Mumtaz Mahal, the wife of Emperor Shah Jahan, died on 28 June 1631, while Shah Jahan, then in the third year of his reign, was on a military campaign in the Deccan (Central India). Mumtaz Mahal was bearing her fourteenth child and was accompanying her royal husband as she had done for the eighteen years of their married life. Mumtaz died in childbirth with her husband at her side.

Arjunand Banu Begam was the daughter of Asaf Khan, a prime minister of the Mughal Court. She married Prince Khurram on 27 March 1612 and was given the title of Mumtaz Mahal by her father-in-law, Jahangir. "Mumtaz Mahal" means "The chosen one of the palace", while Prince Khurram's title "Shah Jahan" means "King of the world". It is reported that during their married life Mumtaz Mahal was a close companion and adviser to her husband.

After her death she was buried in a temporary grave in Burhanpur, where they were encamped. It is said that the Emperor was so striken with grief that he abstained from rich food and wore only the simplest of clothes, and the whole court went into mourning for several years.

The Taj Mahal at sunrise in winter.

The remains of Mumtaz Mahal were brought to Agra within six months of her death and were given another temporary grave at the site where the Taj Mahal was later built. Work on the Taj Mahal must have begun soon after the first anniversary of Mumtaz Mahal's death in 1632.

The name Taj is derived from Mumtaz with the omission of the first syllable (*z* and *j* being interchangeable), hence the tomb of Mumtaz Mahal has come to be known as the Taj Mahal.

Throughout India there are monuments, tombs and pilgrimage centres that have been constructed for the burial of important people and saints. It is believed that a visit to such places enables one to share in the richness of the spirit of the person buried there. The Taj Mahal may have been conceived by Shah Jahan as an *Urs*, or pilgrimage place. In more recent times, the Taj has been eulogised as a monument built in memory of Love, a memorial to years of companionship between an emperor and his beautiful wife. To visit the Taj today is to partake in that spirit and sentiment.

During the reign of Shah Jahan and his descendants, the Taj Mahal was open to the public only on rare occasions

Today the garden has a few trees not of Mughal but of nineteenth-century British origin.

but never to non-Muslims. Apart from the annual memorial service for Mumtaz Mahal, the visits to the tomb by the nobility were akin to a pilgrimage. Prayers, devotional music and recitation of poetry must have filled the air, for it was not a tourist spot but an extravagant dream of an emperor to sanctify his wife's memory and his own.

The location

The Taj Mahal was constructed within a large enclosed garden on the banks of the Yamuna river, which flows due west to east past it. The Yamuna, or Jamuna, is one of five branches that join the sacred river Ganga. It links the cities of Delhi and Agra, and emperors like Shah Jahan travelled on it in large barges and boats.

The Mughal emperors had three capitals, Delhi, Agra and Lahore (now in Pakistan), of equal importance and fame. It is not surprising that Shah Jahan chose this site in Agra to build the Taj, for he could see it from the royal chambers of the Agra fort, which also faces the river. With nothing behind the Taj Mahal, but the river flowing below, the building stands against the sky, as though in a world all of its own.

The land on which the Taj Mahal stands was once a garden belonging to Raja Jai Singh of Amber, a princely state of Rajasthan. It was recorded in the *farman* (decree) of 18 December 1633 that the Emperor Shah Jahan gave the Raja of Amber four royal mansions in compensation for the garden.

The plan of the Taj Mahal complex

The Taj Mahal was planned as a *rauza* (tomb) and an *urs* (pilgrimage centre) and hence the complex includes the tomb, garden, bazar and service area, enclosed by boundary walls.

The whole Taj complex forms a rectangle aligned north

to south measuring approximately 580 (579.12) m. long
and 305 (304.80) m. broad (17.7 hectares in area) (1900 ft
by 1000 ft). The northernmost side of the rectangular
complex is occupied by a square raised platform and the
tomb overlooking the river. There was a riverside
entrance used by the Emperor when he came by barge
from the Agra Fort. In front of the tomb is a square garden
which is subdivided into four by the water channels to
form the *charbagh* or four-portioned garden plan. The
tomb garden and subsidiary buildings are enclosed by a
boundary wall with octagonal pavilions at each corner and
a monumental entrance gateway in the centre of the
southern side. In front of this gateway is the enclosed forecourt of the Jilau Khana or bazar area, servant quarters
and service areas.

(Facing) *The first glimpse of the Taj Mahal.*

The architect of the Taj Mahal

The Emperor Shah Jahan gathered hundreds of master builders and craftsmen from India and West Asia, both Hindu and Muslim, to build the Taj Mahal.

There were many who aspired to be acclaimed as the chief architect of the Taj. Amongst them are Geronimo Veroneo, the Venetian goldsmith, the Turk Ustad Isa, and Ustad Ahmad Lahori.

From literary and inscriptional evidence it is apparent that various master craftsmen were assigned specific work such as designing the dome, garden, inlay, calligraphy, and mason work. They worked as a team, following the model and master plan approved by the Emperor.

Over 20,000 workers were involved in the building activity and temporary settlements were made for them. Indian craftsmen had over ten generations of training in the building of Islamic architecture and had perfected every detail. The closest model for the Taj Mahal had been completed some sixty years before, at Humayun's Tomb in Delhi. Therefore the Taj Mahal is a perfect synthesis of Hindu and Muslim art and expression.

The imprisoned emperor's last view.

The Taj Mahal through Khas Mahal pavilion, Agra fort.

The construction of the Taj

It would be impossible to calculate the cost of building the Taj. Some attempts have been made. The *Badshah Nama* of Abdul Hamid Lahori mentions a figure of Rs.50 lakhs. In 1836 Sleeman was told it cost Rs.3,17,48,028 or £3,174,802 at that time. A local guidebook has priced the priceless Taj at 30 million pounds. It is difficult to estimate how much expenditure was involved, as some materials were presented, others were brought from the Empire and different parts of the world. Craftsmen were paid, but there may have been many labourers and others who were not.

In the *Tarikh-i-Taj Mahal* we are told that the white marble was brought from Makrana, in Rajasthan, the yellow marble from Central India, crystal from China, lapis lazuli from Sri Lanka, jasper from Punjab, onyx from Persia, turquoise from Tibet, coral and mother of pearl from the Indian Ocean.

According to Jean Baptiste Tavernier, a French traveller of that period, to build the Taj Mahal a huge brick scaffold was constructed all around with ramparts on which elephants and oxen hauled the materials.

The entire Taj Mahal took over twenty years to complete. Work began in 1632 and by 1643 the Taj Mahal was ready for the formal annual memorial ceremony, but work on subsidiary parts of the complex were not finished before 1653.

The entrance to the Taj Mahal. The forecourt was occupied by shops and service quarters to meet the needs of the pilgrims and visitors.

The gateway to the Taj Mahal, constructed of red sandstone with white marble inlay and calligraphy.

Entrance to the Taj Mahal

In front of the main gate of the Taj was once the Jilau Khana or bazar, full of shops for the nobility who would have entered this area on horseback or in palanquins. Today parts of this area are occupied by tourist shops and the car park.

The gateway or entrance to the Taj Mahal was built in red sandstone. It is two storeys high, with a large apsidal entrance flanked by two octagonal towers. The red of the sandstone gateway is relieved by the use of white marble inlay work and calligraphy. The marble band of calligraphy has been inlayed in black slate stone with verses

from the Koran. The original doors of the entrance were made of silver, studded with silver rupee coins which was stolen by anti Mughal rebels in 1764. Today the large doors are of brass.

As you enter the gateway, the first glimpse of the Taj Mahal can be seen. From this distance the Taj looks small, framed within the arch of the entrance. From the gateway every step towards the Taj makes the monument appear larger, till its massive proportions become overpowering. So cleverly has the distance between the gateway and tomb been designed, that from the entrance the Taj appears like a tiny, white jewel casket.

The garden

When Shah Jahan built the Taj the garden was full of trees, a mixture of an orchard along with cypress and palm trees and flowers. The flowers were not what you see today, but species of narcissus, iris, tulip and rose. Since it must have been much quieter and greener there would have been more birds and butterflies. It was conceived as the Garden of Eden or Bagh-i-Adam with trees, flowers and water flowing in the channels.

Today the garden has a few trees, a lawn and regimented flowerbeds, not of Mughal but of nineteenth-century British origin. The formal garden today follows the *charbagh* or four-portioned garden plan. The central water channel has an elevated pool in the centre called Haus-i-Kausar. In this axial water channel the reflection of the Taj Mahal can be seen in its perfect symmetrical proportions. From the central pool the water channels flow in

*In the days of Shah Jahan the garden-orchards had
flowers like narcissus, iris and tulips to create the illusion
of the garden of Eden or* Bagh-i-Adam.

*Water channels, glittering in the light, compassing the
greenery, and dividing it into four plots, or the* charbagh
garden design.

four directions, dividing the garden area into four. At the ends of the channel that divides the garden into half, on the east and west side, are the Naubat Khannas or music halls, where music was played on Thursdays and Urs or pilgrimage days.

The water for the channels was hauled up from the river behind the Taj Mahal, the inclination and level of the garden being designed to keep the water constantly flowing. It is suggested that visitors walk around the garden, because every view and angle of the Taj Mahal is worth seeing. There are benches to sit on and the lawns, to encourage you to do just that.

The Mosque and Mihman Khana

As you enter from the gateway and look ahead, to the north, you will see the garden, beyond which is the tomb building in the centre and two detached subsidiary buildings of red sandstone and marble on either side. On the western side is a mosque and on the opposite side is the Mihman Khana, a building constructed to provide symmetrical balance or *jawab* (answer) to the mosque, but with no religious import. Both these buildings have three domes, of which the central one is the largest, and faced with marble. The inlay work on white marble, the painted ceiling and wall panels of the mosque and *jawab* complement the Taj Mahal.

The Taj Mahal

The tomb or mausoleum is perhaps the most beautiful in the world. Its beauty lies in the architectural simplicity, the perfect balance and proportion of the structure. The uniqueness of the building is that it has been constructed in pure white marble. The monotony of the building faced entirely with white marble is enlivened by highlights of inlay and calligraphy in other coloured stones. The gentle white of the building gives it a quality of weightlessness. It is the excellent crystalline character of the marble that captures the subtle changes of Nature's moods and the play of sun and moonlight.

The tomb building has a very simple plan. It is raised on a square terrace platform 5.486 m high and 95 m square, with four minarets approximately 42 m high. Inside, the

The Taj Mahal, seen from within its own gardens.

building has one large octagonal room which houses the tombs of Mumtaz Mahal and the Emperor Shah Jahan. Above the room is a large domed roof. Around the octagonal tomb room is a passage consisting of small rectangular rooms, and this plan is repeated on the floor above. Yet this simple layout of rooms, the harmony of proportions and delicate decorations took generations of experimentation to perfect.

There is a symmetry and balance in the mathematical proportions of the building. The terrace platform is 95 m square, the tomb is 57 m square with the right angles

18

The Taj Mahal from the Agra fort with the river Yamuna in the foreground.

Taj panel near the entrance.

chamfered to form an eight-sided structure. The eight faces of the building are like facets on a gemstone, catching the light in all directions. The height of the building rises to approximately 75 m with the large bulbous dome of a height of 25 m and a diameter of 18 m. Therefore the width of the building is almost equal to its height, and the façade in the centre has the same height as the dome.

The dome, a brilliant architectural achievement, is raised on a large truncated drum, so that the form and volume is never lost, from whichever angle you view the building. The shape of the dome is Persian or more correctly Central Asian in origin but had been experimented with in India in other buildings. The dome emerges from its drum base with a border of inlay design and culminates

(Facing) *A view of the mosque from within the Taj Mahal.*

with an inverted lotus design. Above this is a tapering Kalasa or water pot with the crescent moon on the top. This finial was originally sheathed in pure gold, which was removed by British troops in the nineteenth century.

Below the dome and in line with the drum are placed four cupolas with domed roofs that are of a different shape to the central one. The apex of the dome to the two corners of the central façade forms a perfect triangle.

The dome of the Taj Mahal is a double dome, so termed because it has been constructed with two shells, the inner one forming the roof of the central tomb room and the outer shell visible from the exterior. The double dome was an architectural innovation to correct visual distortion of the interior and exterior appearance of the dome.

Walking on the terrace platform of the Taj Mahal

At the base of the terrace platform, visitors are asked to remove their shoes, this being a requirement for the preservation of the monument and a mark of respect. It is a delight to walk barefoot on the smooth marble pavement, warmed by the sun, and the interiors of the building are always cool.

Once on the terrace, the building takes on yet another dimension. The raised platform provides a beautiful view of the layout of the garden, the water channels and the entrance gateway. The terrace is broad and a walk around the building is recommended. There are four minarets on

One of the two minarets by moonlight.

Terrace view of the river and Agra fort.

the corners of the terrace. Each minaret is built with three storeys, topped with a domed cupola similar but smaller to the ones that rest by the central dome of the main building. The minarets are faced with white marble and the balconies of each storey are supported by delicately carved brackets. Once again the minarets have been constructed at an angle to correct the illusion of a slant or tilt caused by high towers.

From the terrace a good view can be had of the mosque on the left of the main entrance. At the back of the building is the river Yamuna, which curves on the left towards the Agra fort. It was along the river from the Agra fort that Shah Jahan came to visit the Taj Mahal. It was also

24

along this river that Shah Jahan's body was brought from the fort to its final resting place at the Taj Mahal on February 3, 1666.

The building of the Taj Mahal has been constructed in two storeys, each of the four façades having four arched recesses and a large central one. The arches have been decorated in the spandrels with floral inlay designs. The base of the recess has a band of sculptured flower panels in marble, framed by a border of inlay work, the design being continued inside the building. The central opening is almost 33 m high and is framed by a border of black

"A poem in marble inspired by the love for a beautiful woman".

Detail of inscription in panel around the main entrance.

inlaid calligraph of verses from the Koran. The calligraphy has been so designed to correct any optical distortion. There is only one entrance into the tomb building, through the central doorway. Perforated, carved marble screens have been placed in each of the other recesses to allow light to flow into the interior of the building.

The flower is a symbol of life, an appropriate decoration
for a tomb that was built in memory of love.

Detail of the marble screen.

The tomb room

Entering the tomb building there is a stairway leading down to the actual tomb chamber. The real tombs have been kept below, to guard them against violation, theft and other possible forms of disrespect. Directly above this crypt, on the same floor as the entrance, is the tomb room containing the ornate decorated replicas of the tombs of Mumtaz Mahal in the centre and of Shah Jahan beside it.

The tomb room is octagonal in plan, and on four sides, light from the marble screens streams through, in varying intensity as the sun moves over the building, east to west. Along the walls of the tomb room is a band of marble panels carved in low relief of vases full of flowers. The white on white carvings of flowers are a poetic reflection of the colourful flower gardens in the tomb garden outside.

In the centre the tombs are protected by a marble screen which is also octagonal, in harmony with the shape of the room. It is said that the tombs were originally enclosed by a solid gold railing, studded with gems. The railing was removed in 1642 and replaced by the marble screen seen today. The workmanship on the screen is exquisite. The perforated, fretted screen have been carved out of single slabs of marble. Each screen appears like lace, filtering the light as it passes through to the tombs. The white marble screens have a border of inlay work of flower motifs, which culminates in a carved panel with inlaid flowers.

Inlay work, or pietra dura, is a form of architectural decoration perfected in the Taj Mahal. An outline is

(Facing) *The entrance to the tomb room is framed by a border of calligraphy in black inlay work with verses of the Koran.*

28

drawn on the plain marble surface, portions of the design carved out and their exact shapes reproduced in coloured stones and gems, which are embedded into the marble so precisely that the surface remains smooth. In the inlay work on the screen and on the tombs there are as many as sixty different precious and semi-precious stones. A single flower has been created with as many as thirty or forty different gems. Every turn and twist of a petal, leaf and stalk has been formed with the appropriate light and darker toned stones, and the outline and veins of the leaf and petal have been embedded with mother of pearl. The gems used range from topaz, crystal, quartz, diamonds and garnets, lapis luzuli and turquoise, for various shades of dark and light blue, to onyx for greens, jasper and coral and agates for the oranges, reds and browns. In agate gems alone there are a hundred different colours chosen to create the various parts of the flower motifs.

The cenotaphs of Shah Jahan and Mumtaz Mahal.

The cenotaphs and enclosing screen.

The screen took ten years to make.

Close-up of the screen.

The cenotaphs of Mumtaz Mahal and Shah Jahan

Enclosed by the marble screens are the ornately decorated tombs of the emperor and his wife. The cenotaph of Mumtaz Mahal is raised on platform made of a single stone, and decorated with inlaid floral designs. On the cenotaph are Koranic verses in praise of God.

Beside her tomb lies the cenotaph of Shah Jahan, which has a slightly different design in that it is decorated not with calligraphy but bands of poppy flowers, and other motifs of buds and creepers. An inscription on the tomb gives the date of Shah Jahan's death and his titles.

Visitors and pilgrims are asked to walk around the tombs, as there are those who offer prayers and pay their

Detail of inlay work on the marble screen.

The cenotaphs.

respects to the royal couple. The attendant in the chamber recites the words 'Allah-hu-Akbar' ("God is great") which resonates in the vaulted ceiling for as long as thirteen seconds. One can almost hear the echo circling the room again and again. It is said that in the days when the tomb was in full use there were mullahs seated in the chamber to recite prayers throughout the day, the floors were covered with costly Persian carpets, and elaborate lamps lit the room in the evenings. All this has gone and the building is no longer used as it was intended to be.

During the reign of Shah Jahan the expenses for the upkeep of the Taj Mahal were met from the produce of thirty villages and from the profit obtained from shops in the Jilau Khana and sale of fruit from the tomb gardens and orchards.

During the uneasy years after the collapse of the Mughal empire, the Taj Mahal was plundered many times. The silver doors of the gateway were stolen, and inlaid gems were picked and gouged out. During the British Raj, Lord William Bentinck was in favour of bringing down the whole building. Fortunately the scheme seemed to be more expensive than profitable and the idea was dropped. Viceroy Lord Curzon was responsible for laying the garden lawns and seeing to its maintenance. He

brought from Cairo a huge brass lamp that hangs over the tombs.

Today the Taj Mahal is under the protection of the Archaeological Survey of India, which sees to its upkeep and maintenance. Yet urbanization, factories, iron foundries and refineries in the vicinity of Agra have so polluted the air that the white marble is slowly turning yellow. The polluted air and acidic rain that falls and the passage of time is corroding the marble of the Taj Mahal. Public awareness and support have now been alerted for the urgent need to help save the monument from further manmade destruction.

"The builder could not have been of this earth for it is evident the design was given him by heaven" (Shah Jahan).

The flower panels in marble run along the exterior and interior of the base of the building.

Flower detail of the marble panel.

When to visit the Taj Mahal

One could say that any season of the year and any time of the day is a good time to visit the Taj: it always looks beautiful. The best time of year would be from October–November to March when the cool winter air, mist and flowers add to its charm.

Preferably one should see the Taj by full moonlight, at sunrise, between 8 and 10 a.m. and then again at sunset. The pure white marble almost changes in colour and tone with the moods of the season and time of day.

If you cannot spend a full day with the Taj, then you need at least two hours to see it well.

The Taj Mahal is open from sunrise to sunset every day and on full-moon nights it is open till 11.30 p.m.

As many as forty gems were needed to create the inlay motifs.

Inlay work: detail of flower motif.

Mongol to Mughal

Mongol is the name for the nomadic tribes of Transoxiana (between Afghanistan and Russia) and is associated with Timur the Lame of the late fourteenth century. Babur preferred to call himself a Turk and introduced Turki as the court language. Mughal was the Persian version of Mongol and used by Babur's descendants in India as a proud reference to their Mongol ancestors.

Babur

He was born in Ferghana, his father's modest State. He made numerous attempts to capture important States like Kabul and finally entered Hindustan in 1525. After successive attempts against local kings he was able to declare himself the ruler of Hindustan in 1526.

To his credit is the establishment of a dynasty that ruled a large portion of India for about 300 years. Babur was responsible for bringing in original ideas and Persian influences, such as the creation of the formal garden.

Being an adventurous and curious man, Babur's diaries are noted for the precise detail and enthusiasm with which he recorded the new plants, animals and customs of people he encountered in India.

Humayun

Babur's son, Humayun, ascended the throne in 1530, but his reign was disturbed by wars and exile. However, Humayun's exile was to have its influence on Indian art and history, as he sought the help of the Persian Shah and was able to regain his kingdom. On his return he brought with him Persian artists and craftsmen, and many ideas and innovations.

Humayun died in 1556 and his tomb was built in 1564 by his wife Hamida Begum, a Persian princess. This tomb in Delhi was the model for the Taj Mahal, on which Shah Jahan perfected every detail.

Akbar

He was born in Amarkot, now in Pakistan, while his father Humayun was in exile. Akbar ascended the throne at the age of thirteen in 1556 and for some years his regent Bairam Khan looked after the empire. During Akbar's reign the Mughal empire expanded from Bengal in the east to Gujarat in the west.

Detail of inlay.

He was noted for his administrative policies and his diplomatic relationships with Hindu rulers. He married the daughter of the Raja of Amber. During his reign he built the Agra fort, Fatehpur Sikri, while his mother completed Humayun's tomb. Persian along with Hindu artists came to his court and during his reign a synthesis of styles emerged in the fields of architecture, painting, music, language and culture.

Jahangir

He was born of the Hindu wife of Akbar and inherited his father's large empire in 1605. Brought up in the stimulating courts, libraries and studios of Akbar, Jahangir developed a love for painting and architecture, and became an accomplished aesthete. Nur Jahan, Jahangir's wife, tried to maintain a hold on the throne after her husband's death, but retired later to build his tomb in Lahore and left the throne to Shah Jahan.

Shah Jahan and Mumtaz Mahal

Shah Jahan was born on January 5, 1592 to Jodhbhai the Hindu wife of Jahangir and was three quarters a Hindu by birth. He was favoured by his grandfather Akbar and was brought up with a fitting education that groomed him to be emperor. It was during these early years that Shah Jahan

was trained in aesthetics, and developed a love for gems, painting and architecture. As a prince his name was Khurram, but was given the title Shah Jahan meaning 'King of the world'. During his father's reign Shah Jahan proved himself to be an able soldier.

Prince Khurram was first married to a Persian princess. He later married Arjunand Banu Begam, the daughter of Asaf Khan, the prime minister and niece of the reigning empress Nur Jahan, in 1612. This was the marriage that lasted eighteen years and it was Arjunand Banu Begam who was given the title 'Mumtaz Mahal' meaning the 'Chosen one of the Palace'.

The couple had fourteen children, of whom only seven

survived. The favourite was the eldest son, Dara Shukoh. But their third son Aurangzeb succeeded Shah Jahan, after long bitter years of battle and intrigue against his brothers. Aurangzeb declared himself emperor in 1658 during Shah Jahan's lifetime, and kept his father under virtual house arrest till he died in 1666. It was in the palaces of Agra fort that Shah Jahan spent his last years in the care of his favourite daughter, Jahanara.

Shah Jahan has gone down in history as a great builder and an enormously wealthy emperor. Not only did he build the Taj Mahal, he converted the sandstone palaces of Agra fort into marble. He built the Delhi fort and the Jama Masjid in Delhi.

But Shah Jahan will always be remembered for being responsible for the creation of the Taj Mahal, the tomb built in memory of his beloved wife and companion, Mumtaz Mahal.

Agra

Agra became an important city during the Mughal period. During the reign of Akbar, it was one of the three capital cities of the empire.

The Red Fort

Akbar, between 1564 and 1574, started work on the Red Fort. The rampart walls, the Red Palace and the palace of Jahangir reflect the Akbari style of architecture with ornately carved pillars and massive red sandstone structures. Much of this fort was redesigned by Shah Jahan during the period 1636 and 1653. The stamp of Shah Jahan can be found in the delicate white marble structures, inlay work and decorations of the Diwani-i-Khas (Hall of Private Audience) the Khas Mahal, Shish Mahal and the Moti Masjid. It was in the Musamman Burj and Khas Mahal that Shah Jahan spent his last days under virtual house arrest ordered by the reigning emperor, his youngest son, Aurangzeb.

Open from sunrise to sunset.

Tomb of Itimad-ud-daulah

This exquisite tomb on the left bank of the Yamuna river was built by Nur Jahan (Light of the world), the wife of the Mughal emperor Jahangir, for her father Mirza Ghias Beg (between 1622 and 1628). The tomb is small in size but built entirely in white marble, a feature that appeared for the first time and was an inspiration for the building of the Taj Mahal.

This elegant structure is enclosed within a boundary wall and a garden. The tomb is square in plan with a simple layout of rooms. The entire building faced with marble has elaborate inlay work with coloured marble, jasper, cornelian etc. The designs are generally geometric with the cypress tree motif and others.

Sikandra

About eight km. from Agra on the Mathura Road is Sikandar where the tomb of Akbar stands.

The tomb was begun by Akbar but completed during his son Jahangir's reign around 1613. The tomb has an imposing gateway of sandstone and marble inlay work. Within the boundary wall is a square garden with the tomb placed at the centre. Similar to the palaces of Fatehpur Sikri built

(Facing) *The veins and outlines of the leaves are in mother-of-pearl. Other gems used are agate, jasper, lapis lazuli, quartz and garnets.*

by Akbar, the tomb in elevation is pyramidal in shape consisting of three storeys of red sandstone pavilions in tiers. On the top is an open courtyard surrounded by a marble screen containing the tomb of Akbar. This tomb is unique in its departure from the Islamic tomb building (which usually has a domed roof).

The exquisite Itimad-ud-daulah, *built by Nur Jahan, wife of Emperor Jahangir.*

Fatehpur Sikri

Approximately 38 km. south west of Agra is the famous capital city built by Akbar around 1570 called Fatehpur Sikri. Sikri was originally a village associated with a Muslim saint called Salim Chisti. It was to him that Akbar paid respects for forecasting the birth of his son and heirs. It is said that Akbar out of gratitude to Salim Chisti built the city at this site on a natural hillock which later was to house the tomb of the saint.

The city capital, containing palaces, courtyards and secular buildings, is built out of red sandstone quarried from the area.

All the palaces and rooms of the royal city carry the distinguishing feature of Akbar's architectural style, the red sandstone, delicate sculptured relief work, Hindu architectural features like the wide hanging eaves and flat roofed structures. The main buildings here are the Diwan-i-Am (Hall of Audience), Diwan-i-Khas, Panch Mahal, Palace of Jodh Bai, Birbal's Palace and the Jama Masjid with the marble tomb of Salim Chisti.

Numerous factors led to the desertion of this city. However, the beauty of the building and sculpture speak of Akbar's magnificent court and era.

Bibliography

JOHN LALL
Taj Mahal and the glory of Mughal Agra. 1982.
Lustre Press Pvt. Limited.

CARROL (David)
The Taj Mahal. 1972.
New York, *Newsweek*.

BROWN (Percy)
Indian Architecture (Islamic period). 1956.
Bombay, D. B. Taraporevala Sons.

GASCOIGNE (Bamber).
The Great Moghuls. 1971.
New Delhi, B.I. Publications.